7-10

OCEANS ALIVE!

Under The Waves

BROWN
BEAR
BOOKS

Published by Brown Bear Books Limited

An imprint of
The Brown Reference Group Ltd
68 Topstone Road
Redding
Connecticut
06896
USA
www.brownreference.com

ISBN-13: 978-1-933834-62-7

Printed in the United States of America

For The Brown Reference Group Ltd
Project Editor: Tom Jackson
Designer: Lynne Lennon
Picture Researcher: Sean Hannaway
Indexer: Tom Jackson
Design Manager: David Poole
Managing Editor: Tim Harris
Production Director: Alastair Gourlay
Children's Publisher: Anne O'Daly
Editorial Director: Lindsey Lowe

Picture Credits
Front Cover: Shutterstock: Chad McDermott t,
Hiroshi Sato c, Irabel8 b.

Alamy: Kevin Schafer 11; Corbis: Jeffrey L.
Rotman 17; FLPA: Reinhard Dirscherl 12-13t, S.
Jonasson 23, Panda Photo 15b, Albert Visage 14,
Norbert Wu 12-13b, 18, 26-27; Getty Images:
Brandon Cole 16-17; iStockphoto: Brett Atkins
24l, 24-25, 25b, Klaas Lingbeek van Kranen 13,
Charles Masters 19, Simon Podgorsek 6-7, Jose
Tejo 26, Westphalia 27; Natural Visions: Norman
T. Nicoll 10-11; Nature PL: Doug Perrine 22,
David Shale 21; Shutterstock: Angel's Gate
Photography 29b, Rich Carey 9b, Tyler Fox 9t,
Saita Hiroyuki 15t, Irabel8 1b, 3b, Chad
McDermott 1t, 3t, Thomas Payne 6, Kristian
Sekulic 5, 28, 29t, Specta 4, Taiga 20, Jordan
Tan 25t, Yang Xiaofeng 8-9.

Artworks: The Brown Reference Group Ltd.

Contents

Introduction

The oceans cover nearly three-quarters of the surface of the world. People criss-cross them all the time in ships, but few people have been lucky enough to take a look below the waves.

★ Most of the animals in the ocean live in shallow seas or they swim near to the surface where sunlight fills the water.

Tough journey

You are about to explore the surface waters of the ocean. It will be difficult work. Divers need special equipment just to look below the surface and must take all the air they breathe with them.

★ The world's oceans can be divided into zones. Each one has a certain set of conditions.

The sunlit zone

Your journey will take you through the water at the top of the ocean down to about 600 feet (180 meters) below the surface. This area is sometimes called the sunlit zone because the sun's light travels into the water, making it brighter and warmer than the deeper areas of the ocean. There is most light in the few feet below the surface. In deeper water, it is darker because less light is getting through.

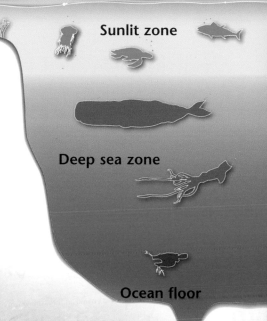

Tidal zone

Sunlit zone

Deep sea zone

Ocean floor

★ Looking up from deep water, the ocean looks blue. That is because the light of other colors cannot travel that far below the surface.

★ BLUE SEA

The light underwater is a different color from in the air. Light from the sun includes all the colors of the rainbow. The shallow water absorbs the red and yellow light first. Only the blue light travels into the deeper water.

Your Mission

Your journey will take you to all corners of the ocean, but you begin in the warm and bright waters around a colorful **coral reef**.

Traveling around

Once you have explored the coral, your mission will then take you far out into the **tropical** ocean. You will come face to face with some of the smallest and largest **organisms** in the ocean.

You will also discover that the ocean does not stand still. Instead, its water flows around the world in swirling **currents**. You will explore one of these ocean currents and see how it affects life in the ocean. It even affects the animals and people who live on shore.

★ The water in this warm part of the ocean has been turned green by tiny **algae** floating in it. Everything in the ocean—including this fish—looks green.

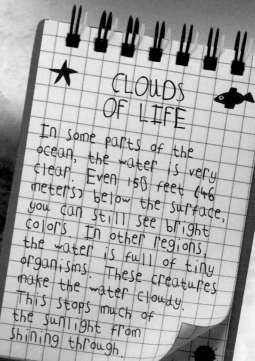

★ CLOUDS OF LIFE

In some parts of the ocean, the water is very clear. Even 150 feet (46 meters) below the surface, you can still see bright colors. In other regions, the water is full of tiny organisms. These creatures make the water cloudy. This stops much of the sunlight from shining through.

★ You will be diving using **scuba** gear. This equipment lets you breathe air from a tank and then breathe out bubbles into the water.

Cool crowd

Then, you will travel north into the cold waters of the North Atlantic. These waters are some of the most crowded in the ocean. We catch many of the fish living there for food. You will dive with huge whales as they also round up large schools of fish to eat. You will find out how a cold ocean can support so many fish.

Ice time

Finally, you will explore the icy world of the Arctic. Even though its surface is frozen, you can dive under the ice of the Arctic Ocean to see what lives beneath. It is now time to set off.

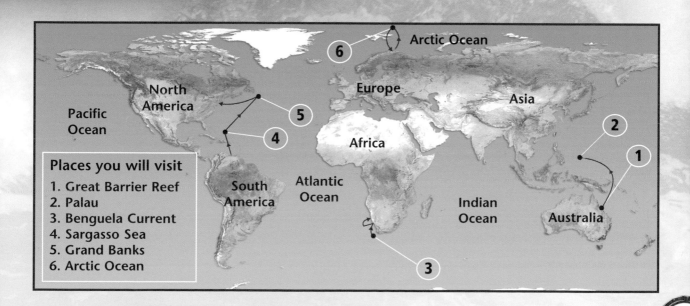

Places you will visit
1. Great Barrier Reef
2. Palau
3. Benguela Current
4. Sargasso Sea
5. Grand Banks
6. Arctic Ocean

Coral Reef

Your first dive will be at the Great Barrier Reef off the northeast coast of Australia, the largest reef on Earth.

Living together

The Great Barrier Reef is so big it can be seen from space! It is actually about 2,500 separate reefs. Each one has been created by millions of corals. Corals are relatives of jellyfish. They live in **colonies** with each coral attached to its neighbors.

Growing rock

Corals have skeletons made of chalky **calcium carbonate**. Over the years, layer on layer of corals have grown on the skeletons of dead corals. Gradually, immense chalky reefs have formed, covered with a thin layer of living corals.

★ Coral reefs have more different types of fish than anywhere else in the ocean.

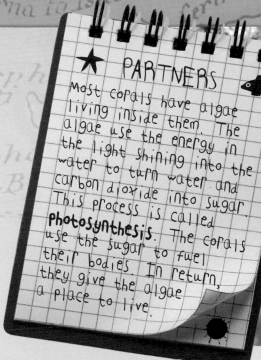

★ There may be two million algae living in a coral as big as your fingernail.

Full of life

You swim slowly over the top of the reef, looking down at the fantastic shapes of the corals. They glow different colors in the sunlight—blue, purple, yellow, and pink— like a colorful underwater garden.

★ Plump parrotfish crunch bits off the corals with their tough teeth.

Floating Creatures

The next day you travel by helicopter to a research ship near the islands of Palau. From there you head out into deep water.

Deep blue

The ocean to the east of Palau is clear and dark blue. The water is very deep. The seabed is more than two and a half miles (4 km) below the surface. Compared to the coral reef, the ocean seems almost lifeless. There are no shoals of colorful fish.

Hidden life

Is there anything there? You take samples of the ocean water from different depths and examine it with a **microscope**. There is very little in the water collected from the deep ocean. However, the water from the sunlit zone contains hundreds of tiny living things. Some are see-through animals that look like shrimp. Others do not look like anything you have seen before. These organisms drift near the surface of the ocean and are known as **plankton**.

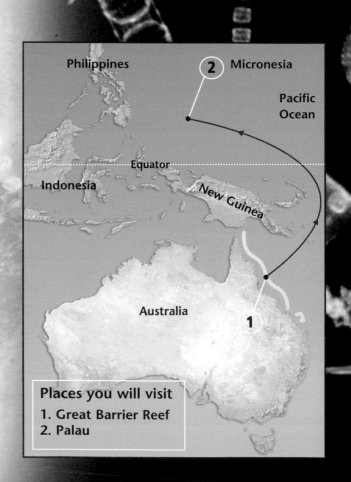

Philippines

2 Micronesia

Pacific Ocean

Equator

Indonesia

New Guinea

Australia

1

Places you will visit
1. Great Barrier Reef
2. Palau

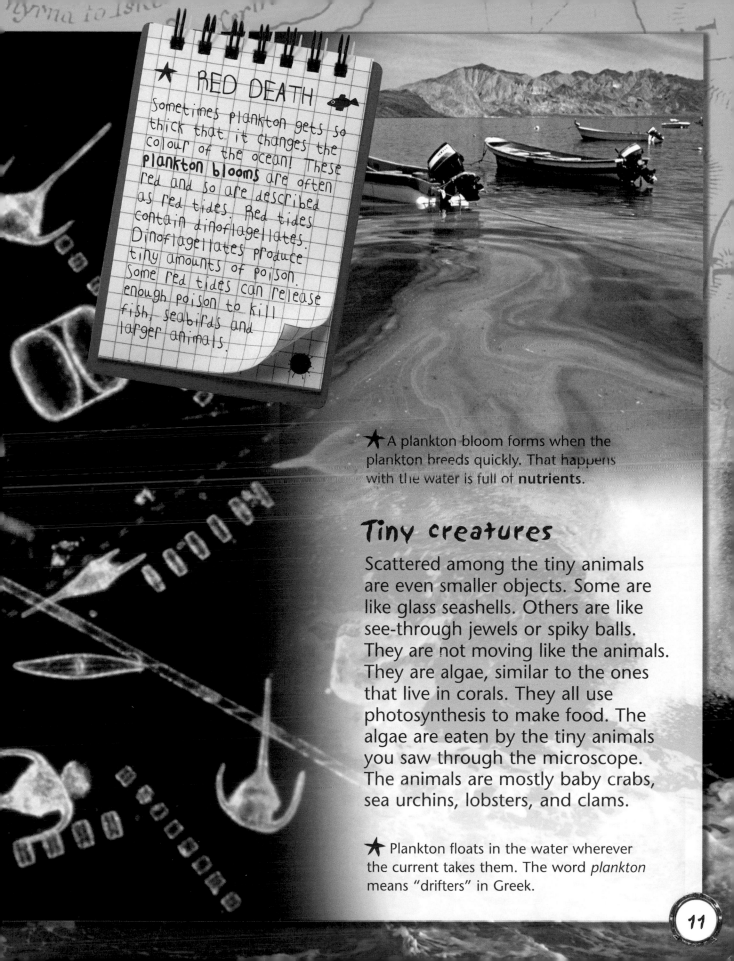

★ RED DEATH 🐟

Sometimes plankton gets so thick that it changes the colour of the ocean! These **plankton blooms** are often red and so are described as red tides. Red tides contain dinoflagellates. Dinoflagellates produce tiny amounts of poison. Some red tides can release enough poison to kill fish, seabirds and larger animals.

★ A plankton bloom forms when the plankton breeds quickly. That happens with the water is full of **nutrients**.

Tiny creatures

Scattered among the tiny animals are even smaller objects. Some are like glass seashells. Others are like see-through jewels or spiky balls. They are not moving like the animals. They are algae, similar to the ones that live in corals. They all use photosynthesis to make food. The algae are eaten by the tiny animals you saw through the microscope. The animals are mostly baby crabs, sea urchins, lobsters, and clams.

★ Plankton floats in the water wherever the current takes them. The word *plankton* means "drifters" in Greek.

Giant Shark

On the voyage back to Palau you discover that the water near to the coast has more plankton in it. And in the distance, seabirds are diving into the sea. There must be food in that area. You decide to take a look.

Food chain

Where there is plankton, there are bigger animals eating it. When you arrive among the birds, you find that they are feeding on small fish. The fish are feeding in an area full of plankton. Most of the plankton is too small to see, but there are some large, floating jellyfish and similar see-through creatures called comb jellies. Wearing your scuba gear, you dive down among them.

★ A whale shark is a filter-feeder. It sieves out bits of food using tiny hooks in the **gills**.

Sudden shock

All of a sudden, a shadow moves overhead. It is a whale shark—the biggest fish in the sea. It is coming at you with a gaping mouth!

Gentle giant

Relax, the shark is not interested in you. It has very small teeth and feeds on plankton and small fish. The shark does not need to look far for food. It just swims through the water with its mouth open.

★ Comb jellies produce flashes of light to attract food. They eat the tiny fish and baby crabs and squids that are floating in the area.

★ SIZE UP

Whale sharks grow 40 feet (12 meters) long and weigh 12 tons (11 tonnes). That is as long as a school bus and heavier than two elephants! The sharks grow this big by eating plankton almost constantly.

Flying Fish!

After your close look at a whale shark, you take a rest back on board the ship. As you gaze into the distance, you see a large, black frigatebird swooping above the water.

★ Flying fish have fins that flap a little like bird wings. However, the extra-long fins are not used for flying—they help the fish glide.

Fins →

Jump for their lives

You climb aboard a speedboat and drive toward the fast-flying bird. As you get closer, you can see that the bird is catching fish—in midair! Its prey are flying fish. They are leaping out of the water to escape another **predator** attacking from below.

Fast flappers

The motor of the speedboat scares the flying fish even more. Suddenly, the ocean is covered with them. Each one moves just above the surface. They are not really flying. The fish beat their tails in the water to make short hops through the air.

High-speed chase

The fish move amazingly fast. Your speedboat is traveling at 37 miles per hour (60 km/h), and the fish are still getting away from you!

Wide ray

You give up the chase and head back to the ship. On the way back, you get the second fright of the day. A huge black creature leaps out of the water ahead of you. Then it falls back with a great splash. It is a manta ray. Rays are flat fish, and the manta is the biggest ray of all. It grows to 12 feet (4 meters) wide. That is as wide as a car is long.

★ Manta rays "fly" through the water by flapping fins that look like wings. The giant rays eat plankton and are harmless to people.

★ SEA STINGER

The Portuguese man o' war is a relative of jellyfish. It floats at the surface of the ocean and is kept afloat by a balloon of air. Under the water, long tentacles trail behind it. The tentacles are covered in stings that kill fish and most other things that swim into them. Once dead, the victims are hoisted into the jelly's central mouth. Portuguese men o' war often give swimmers a painful sting if they drift close to beaches.

Death in the Waves

Plankton are the first link in the ocean's **food chain**. They provide food for nearly all the other animals in the sea. You head to South Africa to investigate other stages in the chain.

Full of life

The waters off South Africa are kept cool by a cold current flowing from Antarctica. This is the Benguela Current. Its water is full of plankton. Fish feed on the plankton, and the fish are eaten by the seals that live on islands along the coast

Tooth

★ SENSORS ON ★
Sharks are amazingly good at tracking their prey through the oceans. They have super-sharp senses, and can hear prey and detect the scent of their blood from more than half a mile (800 meters) away. They also sense the electricity made by an animal's muscles, so they can strike even in total darkness!

★ A great white grows to 20 feet (6 meters), and its razor-edged teeth can slice a seal in half with a single bite.

★ Great whites cannot bite through the bars of the cage, and the metal also affects their electricity sensors.

Cool killer

The seals are not the biggest hunters in these waters. They are preyed on by the ocean's fiercest killer—the great white shark. To be safe, you dive inside a steel shark cage.

Under attack

Soon a shark is drawn to the cage by a bait of raw meat. It attacks from behind you, biting at the steel cage, inches from your head. The bars hold, and a few of the shark's teeth are knocked out. You catch one; it will help you remember the day when you met a great white!

Feeding Zone

Back on board the boat you notice that you are slowly drifting north in the current. You decide to find out where the current will take you.

Cold current

The boat's skipper tells you that the main current is farther out to sea. The sea water is getting colder as you enter the main current. It drops to just 50 °F (10 °C)—too cold to swim without a diving suit. The water has also been turned green by all the plankton in it.

★ The dolphins work together to herd fish. They then take it in turns to rush through the shoal, grabbing a meal.

Crowded with food

You scan the horizon with binoculars. You can see the edge of the current, where the water turns blue again. Nearby you see a huge flock of gannets. These are large diving seabirds that plunge into the green water. They ignore the blue water—all the fish they want are crowded into the current's plankton-rich stream.

Fellow travellers

As you approach the swooping flock, your boat is joined by dolphins. Deeper down you can see a school of tuna fish speeding through the water, too. They are all heading to the same place—an immense shoal of smaller fishes just below the surface. The shoal includes millions of sardines, herrings, and anchovies. You dive among the fish and see a frenzy of activity. The fish dart in all directions as they are attacked from all angles.

★ RISING WATER

The ocean off Namibia is full of life because of an ocean **upwelling**. The wind and Earth's rotation drag the surface water away from the coast. Deep, nutrient-rich water is drawn up from the ocean floor to take its place. The result is an area of ocean filled with plankton and shoals of fish.

★ Gannets spend many days on end soaring high above the ocean looking for food in the water. The birds spend most of their lives far from land.

Sargasso Sea

After looking at what happens when the ocean water is on the move, you head for a part of the ocean that is always calm.

Still water

The Benguela Current is one part of a great swirl of ocean currents called a **gyre**. The gyre moves counterclockwise around the South Atlantic. There is another gyre in the North Atlantic, which flows clockwise. In the middle of each gyre is a calm area of ocean. The calm region inside the North Atlantic gyre is the Sargasso Sea.

Catch the wind

A good way of getting to the Sargasso Sea is to be blown by the wind. Your large yacht sets sail from Venezuela. The wind blows north in this area—and helps to drive the currents in the North Atlantic.

Becalmed

Once you get north of the Caribbean Sea, the wind drops and you enter the calm zone. Old sailing ships avoided this region. Without wind they would get stuck there! Luckily, your boat has a powerful engine so you can keep going all the way to the heart of the Sargasso Sea.

★ The winds that blow you through the Atlantic are called the trade winds because they were once used by merchant ships.

★ A sargassum fish lies hidden among the weeds waiting to ambush smaller fish or shrimp that swim past.

Floating weed

Your instruments show that the sea is warm, very salty, and crystal clear. The yacht is surrounded by brown sargassum weed, which floats in mats on the surface. You dive in to look for the sea's most famous resident—the sargassum fish. It takes you a long time to find one. The fish is camouflaged to look like a pieces of seaweed.

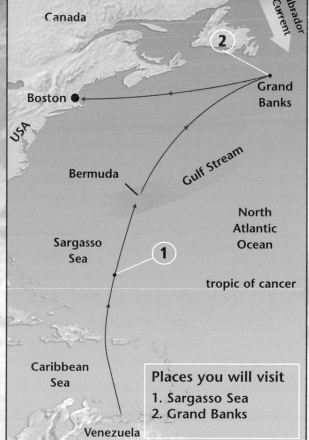

Canada

Labrador Current

2

Grand Banks

Boston

USA

Gulf Stream

Bermuda

North Atlantic Ocean

Sargasso Sea

1

tropic of cancer

Caribbean Sea

Venezuela

Places you will visit
1. Sargasso Sea
2. Grand Banks

Current Clash

From the Sargasso Sea, you head farther north. At Bermuda you board another research ship. You are going to see what happens when ocean currents collide.

Streaming along

From Bermuda you will sail northeast along the warm Gulf Stream. The Gulf Stream runs from the Gulf of Mexico to the North Atlantic. It is a fast current—it flows faster than you can walk. Every second, it moves enough water to fill 5 billion buckets of water! On your voyage you see a leatherback turtle. This is the largest type of turtle. It grows to 6 feet (1.8 meters) long.

★ Leatherback turtles prey on clouds of jellyfish floating in the Gulf Stream and other warm currents.

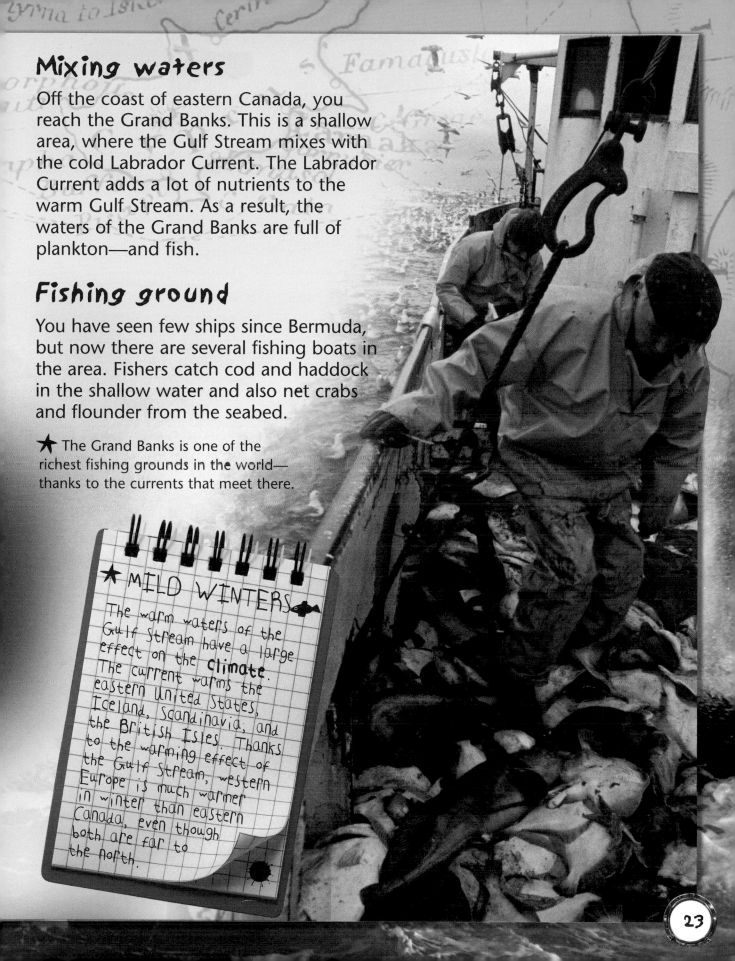

Mixing waters

Off the coast of eastern Canada, you reach the Grand Banks. This is a shallow area, where the Gulf Stream mixes with the cold Labrador Current. The Labrador Current adds a lot of nutrients to the warm Gulf Stream. As a result, the waters of the Grand Banks are full of plankton—and fish.

Fishing ground

You have seen few ships since Bermuda, but now there are several fishing boats in the area. Fishers catch cod and haddock in the shallow water and also net crabs and flounder from the seabed.

★ The Grand Banks is one of the richest fishing grounds in the world—thanks to the currents that meet there.

★ MILD WINTERS

The warm waters of the Gulf Stream have a large effect on the **climate**. The current warms the eastern United States, Iceland, Scandinavia, and the British Isles. Thanks to the warming effect of the Gulf Stream, western Europe is much warmer in winter than eastern Canada, even though both are far to the north.

Whale Watching

You soon discover that the fishing boats are not the only large objects in the water. A enormous humpback whale has just burst through the surface.

★ A humpback breaches—the name for its high jumps out of the water—to create a loud splash. The noise is meant to show other whales how strong it is.

Spring swim

In spring, the whales swim from warm tropical seas to cooler northern waters to feast on the fish. They are huge animals, up to 60 feet (18 meters) long. That's longer than a school bus.

Searching south

You want to use the ship's **submersible** to watch the whales. The captain says you will find large groups of whales to the south—nearer to Boston. Sure enough you soon spot a dozen whales in the water. They are feeding on a shoal of herring just under the surface.

Flipper

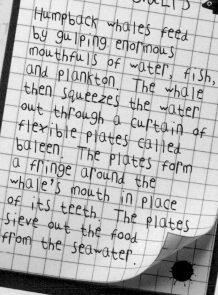

★ A humpback whale surges out of the water after gulping down herring.

Bubble netting

Once in the water, you track the whales with your **sonar** and dive down to get a closer look. One whale is swimming around a shoal of herring, blowing bubbles of air from its mouth. The bubbles form a silvery boundary around the shoal of fish. The "net" of bubbles makes the fish bunch together in a tight ball. The whale then swims up and scoops thousands of them in one gulp.

Frozen Ocean

You go ashore at Boston and catch a plane to Murmansk, a port on the Arctic Ocean in northern Russia. It is so cold here that the ocean is frozen solid.

Icebreaker

The last voyage of your mission will be aboard a ship with a difference—an icebreaker. This huge vessel has a thick, heavy hull that is tough enough to crack the ice covering the Arctic Ocean. The ice is about 10 feet (3 meters) thick and it is slow going.

Always day

You have arrived in late spring. At this time of year, it is daylight all the time in the Arctic—the Sun never sets. (In winter it never rises, and it is night for weeks on end.) The sunlight shines through the ice, and the plankton is blooming underneath. Even in this cold ocean, there is plenty of food for animals. But to see them you will have to dive under the ice!

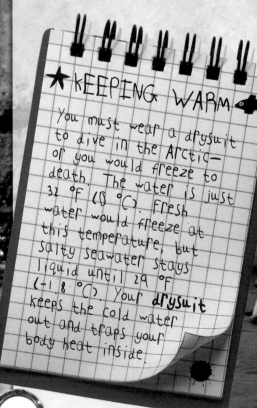

★ KEEPING WARM

You must wear a drysuit to dive in the Arctic—or you would freeze to death. The water is just 32 °F (0 °C). Fresh water would freeze at this temperature, but salty seawater stays liquid until 29 °F (-1.8 °C). Your drysuit keeps the cold water out and traps your body heat inside.

★ Icebreakers are used to open lanes for normal ships. In summer, when the Arctic ice thins, icebreakers can even sail all the way to the North Pole.

★ Seals breathe air, so they make holes in thin ice to breathe through between dives.

North Pole

Area of Arctic Ocean that is frozen all year.

dive site

Greenland

Area of Arctic Ocean that is frozen in winter.

● Murmansk

Russia

Under the ice

Arctic fish are so cold that they swim slowly. But not everything is slow—a seal whooshes past you. You follow the seal and it leads you to a breathing hole in the ice. As it rests, a polar bear's mighty paw reaches in and drags out the seal! As the seal's blood trickles into the water, you decide to head back to the ship.

Lessons We've Learned

You have discovered a lot on your journey through the top of the ocean. Some of it came as a surprise.

Warm and empty

Before you started, you might have thought that the warmest oceans were the ones with most life. Your trip to the coral reef certainly made it look that way. But, away from land, many warm, tropical oceans do not have that many creatures living in them.

Food and light

The things that bring an ocean to life are nutrients and sunlight. The nutrients are stirred up by ocean currents. They are **absorbed** by the **microscopic** algae in the plankton, which use sunlight to make food. The algae then grow and multiply and are eaten by tiny plankton animals. The plankton provides food for fish and all the other animals in the ocean. In some places, this happens all year round. In other places the plankton supply varies with the seasons.

★ A seahorse is a tube-shaped fish that clings upright to seaweeds with its coiled tail, sucking up food from the water.

★ The lion fish lives in coral reefs. Its impressive spines contain a poison.

Moving water

Ocean currents take warm water to the poles and cold water toward the tropics. They make Earth a more comfortable place to live, especially in places like western Europe.

COLD SEA, DRY LAND

Some of the world's driest land is by the ocean. With so much water nearby, how come the land is so dry? The reason is that cold ocean currents run along the coast. In most places wind blowing in from the sea is full of water, which falls on the land as rain. However, a cold current cools the wind out at sea, making fog. So only fog, not rain, reaches land.

Glossary

absorb soak up

algae plantlike living things. Some are tiny, single cells. Others can be very big, such as some seaweeds.

calcium carbonate the chalky white substance in seashells and coral reefs. Calcium carbonate is also the main ingredient in limestone.

climate weather of a place over a whole year

colony group of living things that live together in the same place

coral reef structure built by a large group of corals with chalky skeletons. Corals are small, sea anemone-like animals

current flow of ocean water

drysuit waterproof clothing that keeps a diver dry and warm in the ocean

food chain organization of animals and plants that shows who eats what

gills parts of a fish's body through which it breathes

gyre big swirl of water currents that revolves around an entire ocean

microscope device for looking at things too small to see with the naked eye

microscopic things that are too small to see with the naked eye

nutrients substances that are needed by animals and plants to stay strong and healthy. Proteins, minerals, and vitamins are all nutrients.

organisms living things. All plants, algae, and animals are organisms

photosynthesis process by which organisms use sunlight to turn chemicals into energy

plankton animals, plants, and plantlike organisms, including algae, that drift near the surface of the ocean

plankton bloom very large increase in the number of animals, plants, and plantlike organisms drifting in the ocean

predator an animal that hunts, kills, and eats other animals

scuba equipment that divers use so that they can breathe under water

sonar device that locates things by bouncing sound signals off them

submersible a small submarine designed for short trips. Some can dive to great depths.

tropical of the tropics. The tropics are the hot parts of Earth either side of the equator.

upwelling area of the ocean where ocean currents drag the water up from the ocean floor

Further Information

Books

Awesome Ocean Science!: Investigating the Secrets of the Underwater World by Cindy A. Littlefield. Charlotte, VT: Williamson Publishing, 2003.

Ocean Food Chains by Allan Morey. Minneapolis, MN: Lake Street Publishers, 2003.

Ocean Explorer by Greg Pyers. Chicago, IL: Raintree, 2005.

Web sites

Games and videos from the BBC's Blue Planet site.
http://www.bbc.co.uk/nature/blueplanet/

National Oceanic and Atmospheric Administration Ocean Explorer.
http://oceanexplorer.noaa.gov/

A virtual tour of the Great Barrier Reef.
http://www.nationalgeographic.com/features/00/earthpulse/reef/reef1_flash.html?fs=animals.nationalgeographic.com

A guide to great white sharks from the Discovery Channel.
http://dsc.discovery.com/sharks/great-white-sharks/

Index